HORRiD HENRY'S
Christmas

HORRiD HENRY'S
Christmas

Francesca Simon

Illustrated by Tony Ross

Orion
Children's Books

Horrid Henry's Christmas first appeared in *Horrid Henry Gets Rich Quick*
First published in Great Britain in 1998 by Orion Children's Books
Reissued in paperback in 2008 by Orion Children's Books
This edition first published in Great Britain in 2017
by Hodder and Stoughton

1 3 5 7 9 10 8 6 4 2

Text copyright Francesca Simon, 1998
Illustrations copyright Tony Ross, 1998, 2017

A CIP catalogue record for this book
is available from the British Library.

ISBN 978 1 5101 0204 0

Printed and bound in China

The paper and board used in this book are made from wood
from responsible sources.

MIX
Paper from
responsible sources
FSC® C104740

Orion Children's Books
An imprint of
Hachette Children's Group
Part of Hodder & Stoughton
Carmelite House
50 Victoria Embankment
London EC4Y 0DZ

An Hachette UK Company
www.hachette.co.uk
www.hachettechildrens.co.uk
www.horridhenry.co.uk

For Rafe and Kit McCauley

There are many more
Horrid Henry Early Reader books available.

For a complete list visit:
www.orionchildrensbooks.co.uk
or
www.horridhenry.co.uk

Contents

Chapter 1

Perfect Peter sat on the sofa looking
through the Toy Heaven catalogue.
Henry had hogged it all morning
to write his Christmas present list.
Naturally, this was not the list of
presents Henry planned to give. This
was the list of what he wanted to get.

Horrid Henry looked up from his work. He'd got a bit stuck after: a million pounds, a parrot, a machete, swimming pool, trampoline, and Killer Catapult.

"Gimme that!" shouted Horrid Henry. He snatched the Toy Heaven catalogue from Perfect Peter.

"You give that back!" shouted Peter.

"It's my turn!" shouted Henry.

"You've had it the whole morning!" shrieked Peter. "Mum!"

"Stop being horrid, Henry," said Mum, running in from the kitchen.

Henry ignored her. His eyes were
glued to the catalogue.

He'd found it.

The toy of his dreams.

The toy he had to have.

"I want a Boom-Boom Basher," said
Henry. It was a brilliant toy which
crashed into everything, an ear-
piercing siren wailing all the while.
Plus all the trasher attachments.
Just the thing for knocking down
Perfect Peter's marble run.

"I've got to have a Boom–Boom Basher," said Henry, adding it to his list in big letters.

"Absolutely not, Henry," said Mum. "I will not have that horrible noisy toy in my house."

"Aw, come on," said Henry. "Pleeease."

Dad came in.

"I want a Boom–Boom Basher
for Christmas," said Henry.

"No way," said Dad.
"Too expensive."

"You are the meanest, most horrible
parents in the whole world,"
screamed Henry. "I hate you!
I want a Boom-Boom Basher!"

"That's no way to ask, Henry," said
Perfect Peter. "I want doesn't get."

Henry lunged at Peter. He was an
octopus squeezing the life out of the
helpless fish trapped in his tentacles.

"Help," spluttered Peter.

"Stop being horrid, Henry, or I'll cancel the visit to Father Christmas," shouted Mum.

Henry stopped.

The smell of burning mince pies drifted into the room.
"Ahh, my pies!" shrieked Mum.

Chapter 2

"How much longer are we going to have to wait?" whined Henry. "I'm sick of this!"

Horrid Henry, Perfect Peter, and Mum were standing near the end of a very long queue waiting to see Father Christmas. They had been waiting for a very long time.

"Oh, Henry, isn't this exciting,"
said Peter. "A chance to meet
Father Christmas. I don't mind
how long I wait."

"Well I do," snapped Henry.
He began to squirm his way
through the crowd.

"Hey, stop pushing!" shouted
Dizzy Dave.

"Wait your turn!" shouted
Moody Margaret.

"I was here first!" shouted Lazy Linda.

Henry shoved his way in beside
Rude Ralph.

"What are you asking Father
Christmas for?" said Henry.
"I want a Boom–Boom Basher."

"Me too," said Ralph.
"And a Goo-Shooter."

Henry's ears pricked up.
"What's that?"

"It's really cool," said Ralph.
"It splatters green goo over
everything and everybody."

"Yeah!" said Horrid Henry as
Mum dragged him back to his
former place in the queue.

"What do you want for Christmas,
Graham?" asked Santa.
"Sweets!" said Greedy Graham.

"What do you want for Christmas,
Bert?" asked Santa.
"I dunno," said Beefy Bert.

"What do you want for Christmas, Peter?" asked Santa.

"A dictionary!" said Peter. "Stamps, seeds, a geometry kit, and some cello music, please."

"No toys?"

"No thank you," said Peter.
"I have plenty of toys already. Here's
a present for you, Santa," he added,
holding out a beautifully wrapped
package. "I made it myself."

"What a delightful young man,"
said Santa. Mum beamed proudly.

"My turn now," said Henry,
pushing Peter off Santa's lap.

"And what do you want for
Christmas, Henry?" asked Santa.

Henry unrolled the list.

"I want a Boom-Boom Basher and
a Goo-Shooter," said Henry.

"Well, we'll see about that,"
said Santa.

"Great!" said Henry.

When grown-ups said "We'll see,"
that almost always meant "Yes."

Chapter 3

It was Christmas Eve.
Mum and Dad were rushing
around the house tidying up
as fast as they could.

Perfect Peter was watching a nature programme on TV.

"I want to watch cartoons!" said Henry. He grabbed the clicker and switched channels.

"I was watching the nature programme!" said Peter. "Mum!"

"Stop it, Henry," muttered Dad.
"Now, both of you, help tidy up
before your aunt and cousin arrive."

Perfect Peter jumped up to help.
Horrid Henry didn't move.

"Do they have to come?" said Henry.

"Yes," said Mum.

"I hate cousin Steve," said Henry.

"No you don't," said Mum.

"I do too," snarled Henry.

If there was a yuckier person walking the earth than Stuck-up Steve, Henry had yet to meet him. It was the one bad thing about Christmas, having him come to stay every year.

Ding Dong.

It must be Rich Aunt Ruby and
his horrible cousin.

Henry watched as his aunt staggered
in carrying boxes and boxes of
presents which she dropped under
the brightly-lit tree. Most of them,
no doubt, for Stuck-up Steve.

"I wish we weren't here," moaned Stuck-up Steve. "Our house is so much nicer."

"Shh," said Rich Aunt Ruby. She went off with Henry's parents.

Stuck-up Steve looked down
at Henry.
"Bet I'll get loads more presents
than you," he said.

"Bet you won't," said Henry,
trying to sound convinced.

"It's not what you get it's the thought that counts," said Perfect Peter.

"*I'm* getting a Boom-Boom Basher *and* a Goo-Shooter," said Stuck-up Steve.

"So am I," said Henry.

"Nah," said Steve. "You'll just get horrible presents like socks and stuff. And won't I laugh."

When I'm king, thought Henry, I'll have a snake pit made just for Steve.

"I'm richer than you," boasted Steve. "And I've got loads more toys."

He looked at the Christmas tree.

"Call that twig a tree?" sneered Steve. "Ours is so big it touches the ceiling."

"Bedtime, boys," called Dad. "And remember, no one is to open any presents until we've eaten lunch and gone for a walk."

"Good idea, Dad," said Perfect Peter. "It's always nice to have some fresh air on Christmas Day and leave the presents for later."

Ha, thought Horrid Henry.
We'll see about that.

Chapter 4

The house was dark. The only noise
was the rasping sound of Stuck-up
Steve snoring away in his sleeping bag.

Horrid Henry could not sleep.

Was there a Boom-Boom Basher
waiting for him downstairs?

He rolled over on his side and tried
to get comfortable.

It was no use.

How could he live until Christmas morning?

Horrid Henry could bear it no longer. He had to find out if he'd been given a Boom-Boom Basher.

Henry crept out of bed, grabbed his torch, stepped over Stuck-up Steve – resisting the urge to stomp on him – and sneaked down the stairs.

CR-EEAK went the creaky stair.

Henry froze.

The house was silent.

Henry tiptoed into the dark
sitting room.

There was the tree.

And there were all the presents,
loads and loads and loads of them!

Right, thought Henry, I'll just have
a quick look for my Boom–Boom
Basher and then get straight back
to bed.

He seized a giant package.
This looked promising.
He gave it a shake.

Thud-thud-thunk.

This sounds good, thought Henry.
His heart leapt. I just know it's a
Boom-Boom Basher.

Then he checked the label: "Merry
Christmas, Steve."

Rats, thought Henry.

He shook another temptingly-shaped
present: "Merry Christmas, Steve."

And another: "Merry Christmas,
Steve."

And another.

And another.

Then Henry felt a small, soft, squishy package. Socks for sure. I hope it's not for me, he thought.

He checked the label: "Merry Christmas, Henry."

There must be some mistake,
thought Henry. Steve needs socks
more than I do. In fact, I'd be doing
him a favour giving them to him.

Switch!

It was the work of a moment to
swap labels.

Now, let's see, thought Henry. He
eyed a Goo-Shooter-shaped package
with Steve's name on it,

then found another, definitely a
book-shaped one, intended for
himself.

Switch!

Come to think of it, Steve had
far too many toys cluttering up his
house. Henry had heard Aunt Ruby
complaining about the mess just
tonight.

Switch! Switch! Switch!

Then Horrid Henry crept back
to bed.

Chapter 5

It was 6:00 a.m.
"Merry Christmas!" shouted Henry.
"Time to open the presents!"

Before anyone could stop him
Henry thundered downstairs.
Stuck-up Steve jumped up and
followed him.

"Wait!" shouted Mum.

"Wait!" shouted Dad.

The boys dashed into the sitting room and flung themselves upon the presents. The room was filled with shrieks of delight and howls of dismay as they tore off the wrapping paper.

"Socks!" screamed Stuck-up Steve.
"What a crummy present! Thanks
for nothing!"

"Don't be so rude, Steve," said Rich
Aunt Ruby, yawning.

"A Goo-Shooter!" shouted Horrid
Henry. "Wow! Just what
I wanted!"

"A geometry set," said Perfect Peter.
"Great!"

"A flower-growing kit?" howled
Stuck-up Steve. "Phooey!"

"Make Your Own Fireworks!"
beamed Henry. "Wow!"

"Tangerines!" screamed Stuck-up
Steve. "This is the worst
Christmas ever!"

"A Boom–Boom Basher!" beamed
Henry. "Gee, thanks. Just what
I wanted!"

"Let me see that label,"
snarled Steve.

He grabbed the torn wrapping paper.

"Merry Christmas, Henry," read
the label.

There was no mistake.

"Where's *my* Boom-Boom
Basher?" screamed Steve.

"It must be here somewhere,"
said Aunt Ruby.

"Ruby, you shouldn't have bought one for Henry," said Mum, frowning.

"I didn't," said Ruby.

Mum looked at Dad.

"Nor me," said Dad.

"Nor me," said Mum.

"Father Christmas gave it to me,"
said Horrid Henry. "I asked him
to and he did."

Silence.

"He's got my presents!" screamed
Steve. "I want them back!"

"They're mine!" screamed Henry,
clutching his booty. "Father
Christmas gave them to me."

"No, mine!" screamed Steve.

Aunt Ruby inspected the labels.
The she looked grimly at the two
howling boys.

"Perhaps I made a mistake when
I labelled some of the presents,"
she muttered to Mum. "Never mind.
We'll sort it out later," she said
to Steve.

"It's not fair!" howled Steve.

"Why don't you try on your new
socks?" said Horrid Henry.

Stuck-up Steve lunged at Henry.
But Henry was ready for him.

SPLAT!

"Aaaarggh!" screamed Steve, green
goo dripping from his face and
clothes and hair.

"HENRY!" screamed Mum and
Dad. "How could you be so horrid!"

Chapter 6

"BOOM-BOOM

CRASH!

NEE NAW NEE NAW

WHOO WHOOO WHOOO!"

What a great Christmas, thought
Henry as his Boom–Boom Basher
knocked over Peter's marble run.

"Say goodbye to Aunt Ruby,
Henry," said Mum.
She looked tired.

Rich Aunt Ruby and Steve had
decided to leave a little earlier than
planned.

"Goodbye, Aunt," said Henry.

"Goodbye, Steve. Can't wait to see
you next Christmas."

"Actually," said Mum, "you're staying the night next month."

Uh-oh, thought Horrid Henry.